The KidHaven Science Library

Molecules

Titles in The KidHaven Science Library include:

Chemical Reaction
Cloning
Electricity
The Extinction of the Dinosaurs
Genetics
Gravity
The Immune System
The Internet
Light
The Mars Rovers
Microscopes
Molds and Fungi
Motion
Plate Tectonics
Space Travel
Thunderstorms
Tornadoes
Volcanoes
Weather

The KidHaven Science Library

Molecules

by Bonnie Juettner

KIDHAVEN PRESS

An imprint of Thomson Gale, a part of The Thomson Corporation

THOMSON

GALE

Detroit • New York • San Francisco • San Diego • New Haven, Conn. • Waterville, Maine • London • Munich

For more information, contact
KidHaven Press
27500 Drake Rd.
Farmington Hills, MI 48331-3535
Or you can visit our Internet site at http://www.gale.com

LIBRARY OF CONGRESS CATALOGING-IN-PUBLICATION DATA

Juettner, Bonnie.
   Molecules / by Bonnie Juettner.
      p. cm. — (The Kidhaven science library)
   Includes bibliographical references and index.
   ISBN 0-7377-2076-X

Printed in the United States of America

Contents

Chapter 1

Atoms and Molecules

Molecules are tiny particles of **matter**, too small for the human eye to see. They are made of even tinier particles, called **atoms**. Atoms are made of even smaller particles. These are called **protons**, **neutrons**, and **electrons**. Everything in the world— humans and other animals, plants, rocks, water, air—is made of these tiny particles.

Elements

If everything in the universe is made of atoms and molecules, why are there any differences between substances? Why can people breathe oxygen but not gold? Why can people eat salt but not silver? The reason is that not all atoms are identical. They vary depending on how many protons they contain. A proton is a tiny particle with a positive electric charge. Scientists know of more than one hundred kinds of atoms, each with a different number of pro- tons. Every type of atom is called an **element**.

Scientists have made a chart of all the elements. It is called the periodic table of the elements. In the periodic table the elements are listed in order of how many protons they have. The number of protons in one atom of an element is called its atomic number. For example, the first element in the

In this computer illustration, electrons orbit the center, or nucleus, of an atom.

periodic table is hydrogen. Each atom of hydrogen has one proton, so hydrogen's atomic number is one. Although protons are very tiny, the number of protons an element has can make a big difference in its properties. Neon (Ne) has ten protons, is a gas, and is used to make neon signs and certain kinds of lasers. Sodium (Na), with eleven protons, is a solid that most people know as salt.

Compounds and Mixtures

When two or more different kinds of atoms join, or bond, the new substance is called a **compound**.

Each water molecule in this illustration is made up of one oxygen atom (green) and two hydrogen atoms (white).

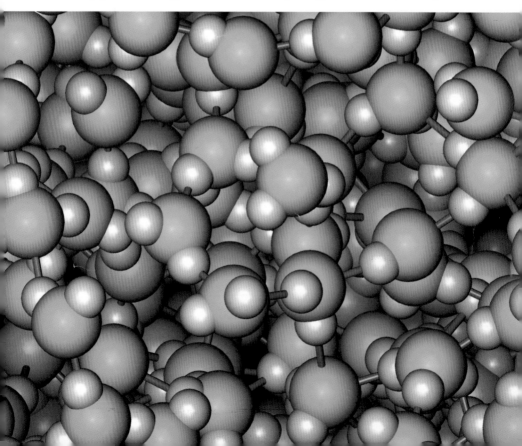

Although a compound is made of two or more ingredients, it is a different substance from its ingredients. Bread is an example of a compound. It is made of flour, yeast, sugar, and water. But a piece of bread cannot be separated into flour, yeast, sugar, or water. It is a different substance altogether.

The smallest possible quantity of any compound is a molecule. For instance, a water molecule contains two hydrogen atoms and one oxygen atom. This is why scientists often refer to water as H_2O. There are billions of water molecules, and billions of hydrogen and oxygen atoms, in a single drop of water. But scientists still call water H_2O no matter how many molecules are in a particular amount of water. They name the molecule according to the smallest amount

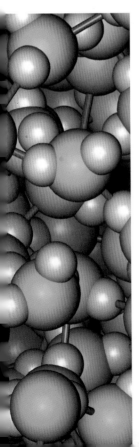

of water it is possible to have in one place—a molecule-sized amount.

The smallest possible amount of any element, even when it is not part of a compound, is also a molecule. The number of atoms that make up a molecule of each element varies. Helium molecules contain just one atom of helium. However, many elements, such as hydrogen, nitrogen, and oxygen, form molecules that consist of two or more atoms that have bonded together. For example, O_2 stands for one oxygen molecule made up of two oxygen atoms bonded together.

Atoms and Molecules

In a **mixture**, the different ingredients put together do not make a new, different substance. The ingredients stay next to each other, but they do not combine chemically. They are like a tossed salad. Unlike the ingredients in bread, the ingredients in a salad can be separated from each other again.

Both mixtures and compounds occur in nature. Earth's air is a mixture. It includes nitrogen molecules (N_2) and oxygen molecules (O_2). It also includes water molecules (H_2O). Water molecules separate from the rest of the air very easily, as rain or dew.

Chemical and Physical Changes

The formation of a compound is a chemical change. A chemical change occurs when one substance is changed into another. When wood burns, for example, a chemical change takes place. The wood turns into ashes and smoke. Another chemical change occurs when metal rusts after being exposed to water. Scientists call chemical changes reactions. When a chemical change occurs the atoms in the reacting substances recombine to form different molecules. The carbon (C) in burning wood, for instance, reacts with oxygen (O_2) in the air. The two substances bond together to form another, a gas called carbon dioxide (CO_2).

The formation of a mixture, on the other hand, is a physical change. A physical change occurs

Physical vs. Chemical Change

A mixture of chopped wood and shredded paper is added to a fire pit. Although the physical properties of the wood and paper have changed, the molecules they are made of remain the same. This is a physical change.

When the fire is lit, carbon molecules from the burning wood and paper enter the air and bond with oxygen, creating carbon dioxide and smoke. This is a chemical change.

Carbon Dioxide Molecules

when a physical property changes but the substance remains the same. For example, if a piece of wood is cut in two, both pieces are still wood. When a physical change occurs, the molecules remain the same as before. Their atoms do not recombine to form different molecules.

The States of Matter

One type of physical change is a change in the state of matter. This happens, for instance, when a solid melts into a liquid, like when a chocolate bar left

A solid may become a liquid, such as when ice cubes melt (inset). As well, a liquid may become a gas, such as when water from a geyser turns into steam.

in a car melts in the hot sun. It also happens when a liquid becomes solid, like when Jell-O becomes firm in a refrigerator. And it happens when water boiled on the stove rises out of the pan as steam.

Heating and Cooling

Changes in the state of matter do not cause the atoms to separate and recombine into different molecules, as they would if a chemical change were taking place. A change in the molecules does take place, but it is a change in temperature. When a substance changes from one state of matter to another, the temperature of its molecules must increase or decrease. If the temperature increases, the molecules get warmer and gain energy. They move faster. If the temperature decreases, the molecules get cooler and lose energy. They move more slowly. When water molecules lose energy, or get colder, eventually the molecules will be moving so slowly that the water will become a solid. It will freeze into ice. If water molecules gain energy, or warm up, eventually they will be moving so fast that some molecules will break off from the rest as steam (which is a gas). Either way, each molecule of water, whether it takes the form of ice, water, or steam, is still made of two hydrogen atoms and one oxygen atom. It is still H_2O. So state of matter changes are physical changes, not chemical ones.

Both chemical and physical changes are a part of daily life. Thinking about solids, liquids, and gases that people encounter every day, one can easily see how they differ. To share a soda with a friend, all one has to do is pour the soda into a glass. But to share a chocolate bar, it is necessary to apply force by breaking the chocolate into pieces. This shows that unlike liquids, solids hold their shapes very well. This is just one example of the many differences between the states of matter.

Chapter 2

Solids

In everyday life people are surrounded by solid objects. The homes people live in, the foods people eat, the tools people use, all are made of solid materials. Solids are one of five states of matter.

What makes solid materials so useful is that people can rely on them to keep their shape. For example, a pencil can be held in a hand. It does not flow all over that hand, creating a sticky mess. Pieces of it do not float away into the air and blow away in the breeze. When a handful of pencils is dropped on the floor, the pencils can be easily picked up. They do not leave a stain on the carpet, as they would if they were made of liquid. Why do solids hold their shape so well?

Solids Stick Together

Solids hold their shape because molecules in a solid stick together. Molecules in solids are held together the same way that magnets stick to a refrigerator. This happens through attraction of positive and

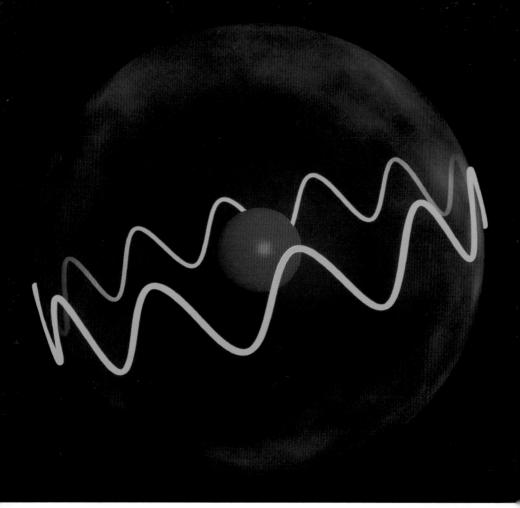

In this illustration of a hydrogen atom, a proton (pink) stays in the nucleus, while an electron orbits the nucleus in a wavy path called an electron cloud.

negative charges. Remember that each atom contains protons, neutrons, and electrons. Protons have a positive charge. Neutrons are neutral. Electrons have a negative charge. The protons in an atom remain in the center, or **nucleus**, of the atom, along with the neutrons. The electrons, however, move around the nucleus in what scientists call an electron cloud.

Usually an atom has an equal number of protons and electrons. The positive charges in the protons and the negative charges in the electrons cancel each other out. This gives the atom a neutral charge, meaning it has no charge at all. Sometimes, however, an atom gives up an electron to another atom. The two atoms are then called **ions**, and they each have a charge. The atom that gave up the electron has a positive charge because now its protons outnumber its electrons. The atom that gained the electron has a negative charge because now its electrons outnumber its protons. Positive and negative charges are attracted to each other, so the two atoms are held together. The force holding them together is magnetism. Because the atoms have become ions, the bond holding them together is called an ionic bond.

Another type of bond, a covalent bond, is formed when atoms share an electron. In this case neither atom becomes an ion. The two atoms stick together because each is attracted to the electron they share.

Properties of Solids

Because the molecules in solids are attached to each other by bonds, they cannot move around. They remain tightly packed together. In most solids, the molecules are packed in regular patterns, making a crystal. The molecules in sugar and salt are arranged in a crystal pattern. Even when they break, crystals form regular shapes. A sugar cube will break into hundreds of tiny sugar granules, each one the same size and shape as the others. Some solids, like glass and most plastics, have molecules that are held together in a random arrangement. These solids even break into random shapes. A dropped glass will shatter into many pieces, none of which may match any of the others. The edges of these shapes often have sharp points.

Because their molecules are packed closely together and stay in one position, solids have certain properties liquids and gases do not have. They will hold their shape unless a physical force makes

This image shows a pile of sugar crystals magnified many times their normal size.

Solids, such as clay, will hold their shape unless a physical force presses them into a new shape.

them change it. The lead in a pencil point, for instance, will hold together unless someone presses down too hard while writing, forcing the tip to break off. Some solids, like the pencil lead, are brittle. Others, like clay, are soft and can be worked into new shapes. Even a soft solid like clay, however, will not change its shape unless a physical force acts on it and presses it into a new shape.

Just as solids have definite shapes, they also have definite volumes. Volume is the amount of space something takes up. For example, the parts of a bicycle will always take up the same amount of space. The handlebars, seat, and wheels can be removed for packing and shipping. But the parts of the bicycle will always have the same volume, even if someone arranges that volume into a new shape.

When the sun shines on icicles, its heat breaks the bonds that hold the molecules together and they become a liquid.

Just as the parts of the bicycle have the same volume when they are rearranged, they also have the same weight. Weight is based on density. It has to do with how closely, or densely, the molecules in a substance are packed together. Like the shape and the volume, the density of a solid does not change unless a physical force makes it change.

State of Matter Changes

The molecules in solids are held tightly together by ionic and covalent bonds. Before a solid can change to another state of matter, something must happen to break those bonds. Physical force will not break the bonds in a solid. Though it is possible to use physical force to break a chocolate bar into many tiny pieces, each piece will still be solid. To melt the chocolate bar into chocolate syrup it is necessary to use something other than physical force. That something is energy. Since heat is a form of energy, people can provide energy to a solid by heating it. This is what cooks do when they heat food on a stove or in an oven.

What happens to molecules in a solid when they are heated? Heat gives them energy to break the bonds that hold them together. Once these bonds are broken, molecules can change position. They can flow past each other without sticking together. They still make up the same substance as before. But now that substance melts and becomes **fluid**.

Chapter 3

Fluids

To be fluid, a substance must be able to flow. Two states of matter are fluid: liquids and gases.

Fluidity

Liquids and gases have something in common that makes them very different from solids. Their molecules are not bonded together in fixed positions as molecules in solids are. Instead, molecules in liquids and gases can flow past each other. This ability to flow is what makes liquids and gases fluid.

Why can molecules in liquids and gases flow? In liquids, molecules have a strong attraction for each other. Since they are not bonded together, they can move from their positions. But because they are attracted to each other, they will not move very far. In gases, however, the molecules do not attract or repel each other. The molecules in gases are neutral, so the molecules in gases can move freely. For example, if someone opens an outside door in winter, the cold air from outside will come in and the warm air from inside will go out. In fact, the only thing that keeps earth's air from traveling into space is gravity.

Shape of Liquids

Because the molecules in liquids and gases are not in fixed positions, they rearrange themselves to take on the shape of whatever container they are placed in. Liquid poured into a glass takes on the shape of the glass. Liquid poured into a test tube takes on the shape of the test tube. A gas can also take on the shape of a container, such as a balloon, if it is sealed. If the container is opened, though, the molecules of the gas spread out into the air.

Liquid mercury forms droplets like these because the molecules have a strong attraction for each other.

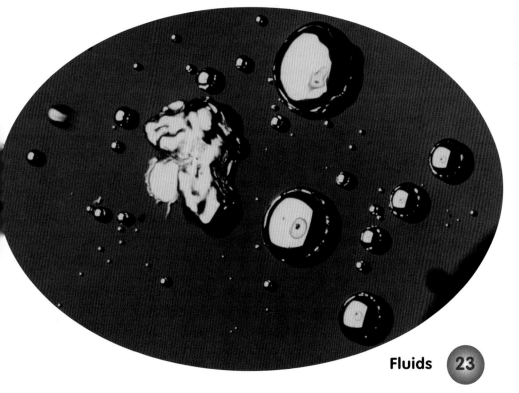

The molecules in the liquid metal this factory worker is pouring will rearrange themselves to take on the shape of the container.

The ability to take on the shape of a container is one characteristic that liquids and gases have in common. However, there is an important difference between them. Liquids, like solids, have an unchanging volume. Although liquids can be poured from container to container, taking on different shapes, the same amount of a liquid will always take up the same amount of space. If milk is poured from a short, fat glass into a tall, skinny glass, its shape will change but its volume will remain the same.

Shape of Gases

Gases, on the other hand, do not have an unchanging volume. If a gas is released from a smaller container into a larger one, it will expand to take up the increased space. This does not mean there are more molecules in the gas than there were before. The number of molecules remains the same. And the molecules do not get bigger. So how can the gas expand to take up more space? Something must increase in size. Something does. What grows is the amount of empty space between the molecules. Because molecules of a gas are not attracted to each other, they drift apart, leaving empty space between them. (The space may not be completely empty. It may contain molecules of other substances. But it is empty of molecules of that particular gas.)

As molecules of the gas drift apart, they mix with other gases. They can mix with oxygen, nitrogen, water vapor, and other gases that make up the air we breathe. There are billions of gas molecules in every cubic inch of air. When a container of gas is opened and the gas is released, its molecules will move around until the gases in the room are evenly mixed. All gases in our atmosphere move around and mix together this way. As a result, the molecules of a gas that is released in one location, such as a breath exhaled by a human, will eventually make their way around the world. Every day everyone on earth breathes in molecules that were once breathed by every other person who has ever lived on our planet.

Because gas molecules will spread out into the available space, people can increase the volume of a gas by releasing it into a larger container. But people can also decrease the volume of a gas. To do this it is necessary to push the molecules of the gas closer together, decreasing the amount of empty space between molecules. This is called applying pressure. If the gas were in a balloon, one could apply pressure by squeezing the balloon to make it take up a smaller space. Balloon artists do this when they make balloon sculptures. But what happens

Gas Compression

Unlike solids and liquids, gases can be pressed into a small space. Because the air inside a scuba tank (right) is compressed, the scuba tank holds more air than a rubber balloon (left).

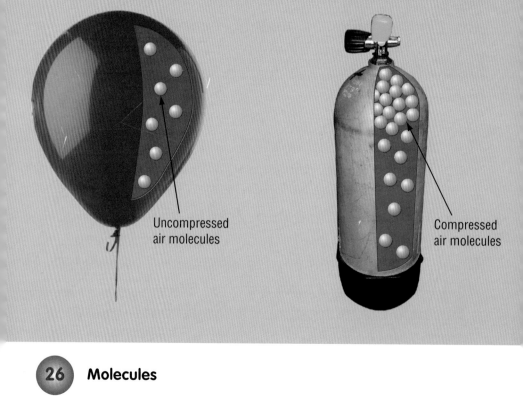

Uncompressed air molecules

Compressed air molecules

if the balloon is squeezed too hard? The pressure inside the balloon will increase so much that the balloon will pop.

It is relatively easy to push the molecules of a gas closer together to make it take up less volume. Because this is so, gases are said to be compressible. This means they can be pressed into a small space. People compress oxygen when they store it in canisters to be used by hospital patients or scuba divers. Although gases are easily compressible, solids and liquids are not. Gas's compressibility is one of the characteristics that makes it different from other states of matter.

Changing States of Matter

Like solids, liquids and gases can change to other states of matter. Changes in the state of matter always involve adding energy or taking energy away. For example, a liquid can change to a solid or a gas. Applying energy in the form of heat gives the molecules in a liquid enough energy to move around freely. When this happens the liquid turns into a gas. This process is called evaporation because the liquid becomes a vapor, or gas. Boiling a liquid causes some of it to evaporate into the air. But liquid can also evaporate because of the heat of the sun. Earth's clouds are partly formed by water evaporating out of the oceans.

Cooling a liquid, or taking away heat energy, will cause it to freeze into a solid. Cooling a gas will cause it to change into a liquid. This process is called condensation. In each case energy is taken away from molecules, causing them to move more and more slowly. Most substances become more dense if they change from a gas to a liquid, or from a liquid to a solid. That is because their molecules get closer together as they lose energy. However, this is not true for every substance.

Water vapor is less dense, with its molecules spread farther apart, than liquid water. But water in its solid form, ice, is also less dense than liquid water. Why? The water molecules in ice are attached to each other by hydrogen bonds. These bonds form in a way that places the molecules farther away from each other than they were when the water was liquid. As a result there is even more empty space between molecules of ice than there is between molecules of liquid water. That is why ice floats on water. If ice were not less dense than water, it would sink to the bottom of lakes in winter. Eventually more and more layers would freeze and sink until

In nature, water can be found as a solid (ice), gas (clouds), and as a liquid.

the lake was solid ice. Fortunately for fish and other aquatic animals, ice remains on top of lakes, insulating the liquid water below from the cold.

Water is unusual in another way as well. In nature it can be found as a solid, a liquid, and a gas. It is the only substance on earth that can be found in these three states at temperatures that are normal for our planet. Scientists working in labs, however, can produce temperatures that are hotter and colder than would ever occur naturally. While working with matter at extreme temperatures, scientists discovered two other states of matter.

Chapter 4

Extreme States of Matter

Many people know of only three states of matter: solid, liquid, and gas. These are the states of matter encountered in daily life. However, scientists know of two others, **plasma** and **Bose-Einstein condensates** (BEC). It took scientists a long time to discover these forms of matter. They exist only at extreme temperatures. Plasma exists at temperatures as hot as the sun. BEC requires temperatures almost as cold as absolute zero.

Plasma

Plasma is the most common state of matter in the universe. More than 99 percent of the universe is made of plasma. Stars are made of it. So is the center of the sun. On earth, plasmas are harder to find. They occur in lightning, which reaches temperatures as hot as the sun. Plasmas also occur in auroras (sometimes called northern lights and southern lights). Auroras are caused by solar wind, a plasma that travels to earth from the sun.

Plasma is a gas. But it is not like other gases. It is so hot that its atoms have become ionized. Unlike the ionic bonding that takes place in a solid, ions in a gas only form at extremely high temperatures. When a gas is heated to 18,032 degrees Fahrenheit (10,000 degrees Celsius), its molecules move so fast

Plasmas occur in lightning, which can be as hot as the sun. They also occur in the Aurora Borealis (inset), or northern lights.

that they collide and break into atoms. Then the atoms collide, electrons are knocked off, and ions form. Instead of creating strong ionic bonds, as they would at lower temperatures, the atoms and electrons are able to move freely.

Plasma is sometimes referred to as ionized gas or electrified gas. Its charged particles make it different from other gases. Gases are not good at conducting electricity. They are better at blocking the flow of electricity. Plasma, on the other hand, can conduct electricity. Its moving ions and electrons form an electric current. Fluorescent lights used in many classrooms contain plasma. Surprisingly, they are not hot to touch. Fluorescent bulbs radiate much more light than heat. Flat screen televisions and computer monitors also use plasma.

Absolute Zero

While plasma forms at extremely hot temperatures, BEC can only form at extremely cold temperatures. The coldest imaginable temperature is absolute zero, the complete absence of heat. At this temperature atoms stop moving. Scientists do not think it is possible to cool any substance down to absolute zero. However, to make BEC they must cool a substance down to three-billionths of a degree above absolute zero.

In 1995, scientists found that when atoms are cooled enough, they do something unusual. They

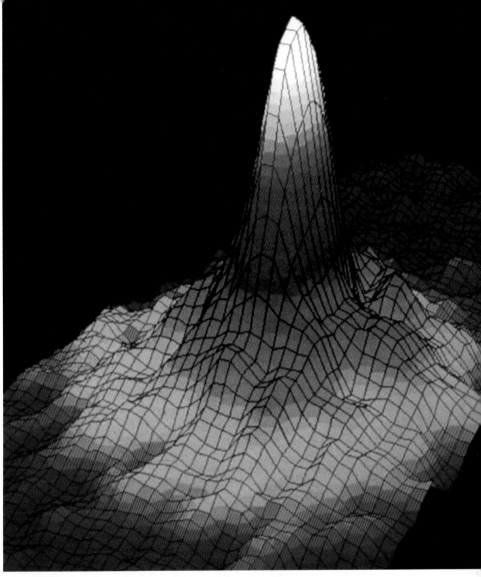

The blue and white peak on this graph represents a Bose-Einstein condensate of rubidium atoms cooled to three-billionths of a degree above absolute zero.

all join together into what some call a superatom. Then they act as if they were one atom, rather than several. This superatom is a different state of matter. Its molecules are not connected with electron bonds, as the molecules of solids are. They do not

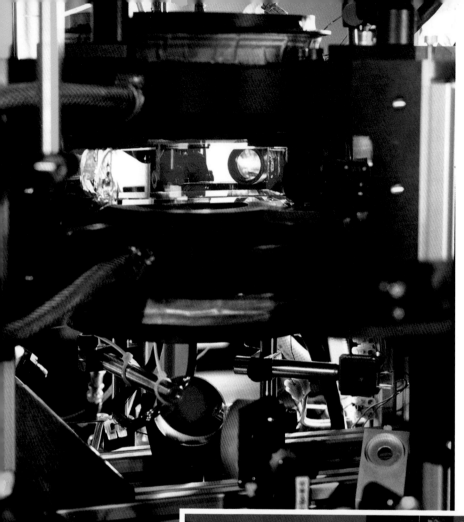

To create BEC, scientists use a magnetic atom transporter (above) to transfer the extremely cold rubidium atoms from one vacuum chamber (right) to another.

 34 **Molecules**

slide past or away from each other, as the molecules of fluids do. Instead, they all occupy the same space. This sounds impossible, and in everyday life, it is. Several chairs cannot occupy the same space. Ordinarily, one atom could not occupy the same space as another atom. But BEC is not formed in ordinary conditions but in extraordinary, incredibly cold conditions.

To make BEC, scientists started with a gas called rubidium. They trapped atoms of rubidium using lasers to surround them. They also bombarded the atoms with light. The light bounced off the atoms, taking heat energy away with it.

How could light take heat away, rather than adding heat to the atoms as it normally would? The laser trap forced the light and atoms to behave in an unusual way. It forced the atoms to slow down. When the atoms slowed down, they also cooled.

Eventually the atoms reached ten-millionths of a degree above absolute zero. But this was still much too hot to create BEC. At this point the scientists turned off the lasers and kept the atoms in a magnetic trap. Warmer atoms were allowed to leap out of the trap, leaving behind the coldest atoms.

When enough atoms reached a cold enough temperature, BEC formed. It was very fragile, though. It could not remain in the BEC state for more than about twenty seconds. (Scientists can now keep BEC in place for a few minutes.) BEC looks a little like a cherry pit, except that it has only about one-fifth the thickness of a sheet of paper. Because BEC is so different from other states of matter, scientists are learning much by studying it. They are understanding more about how the tiniest particles of matter work. In the process they are inventing new technology to do things that were never before possible.

Molecule-Sized Technology

Scientists are not sure exactly how BEC can be used, but knowledge gained by studying BEC has already brought results. In 1999 a team at Harvard used the technology to slow, and then completely stop, a beam of light. Light normally travels at 300,000 km per second (186,000 miles per second). Previously scientists could redirect light or use its energy. They had never before caused light to stop moving.

Some scientists think that the study of BEC also may lead to the invention of new tools that can be used for nanotechnology. Nanotechnology involves moving individual atoms and molecules to make very tiny structures. These structures are about one ten-thousandth the width of a human hair and three to five times as large as a single atom. They can only be seen under a special, very powerful microscope. They are called nanostructures because they are as small as a nanometer, which is one-billionth of a meter.

Study of BEC has already led to development of an important new tool. While studying BEC, scientist Wolfgang Ketterle invented the world's first atomic laser. This laser does not give off concentrated light, as other lasers do. Instead it projects atoms of matter. Light lasers can be used to do

These tiny gears and cogs magnified many times their normal size could be used to design machines that would deliver drugs or fight cancer inside the body.

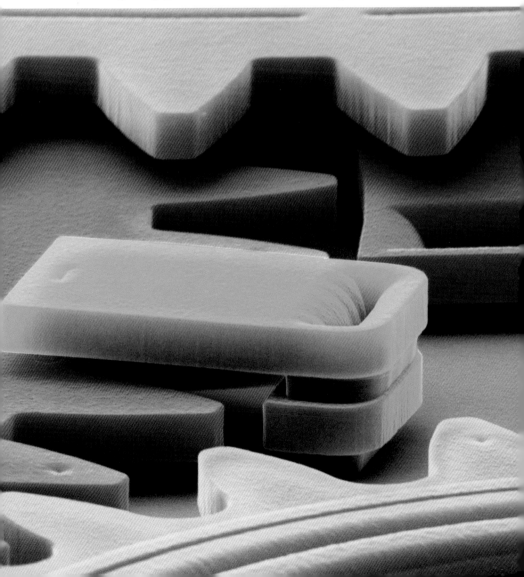

extremely accurate cutting. For example, light lasers are used for eye surgery. Atomic lasers, however, might be useful for very precise building. They could be used to build complex nanostructures.

Why would anyone want to make something so small? Scientists believe that it may be possible to use nanotechnology to improve life in all kinds of

Computer art shows a nanorobot using a laser to destroy bacteria inside a blood vessel.

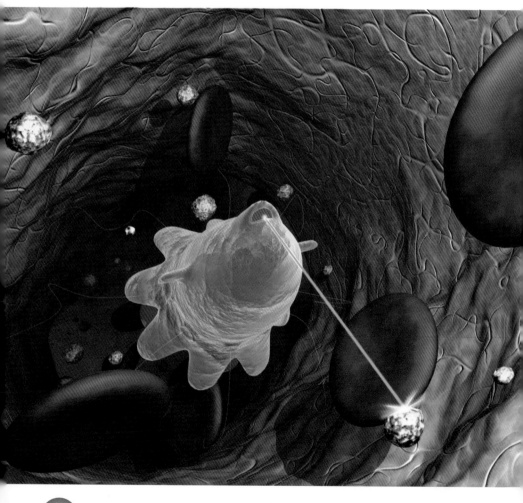

ways. Nanotechnology could be used to make stronger or more flexible metals, smaller computer chips, or even food and water. Some scientists hope to make nanorobots that could travel into the human body to take apart cancer cells or destroy viruses. It might even become possible for nanorobots to help the environment by cleaning up oil spills or repairing damage caused by air pollution.

Scientists still have much to learn about molecules. In 2004 *another* new state of matter was discovered. It is called femionic condensates and is related to BEC.

This kind of research may seem to have little in common with the everyday lives of most people. The average person may not even realize that such a thing as BEC could ever exist. However, the study of molecules and states of matter may lead to important discoveries affecting daily life. Through their research, scientists may learn more about the human body, the atmosphere, and energy. All of these are made of molecules.

Glossary

atom: Tiny particles that all matter is made of.

Bose-Einstein condensate: The fifth state of matter, achieved when atoms fuse together at temperatures near absolute zero.

compound: A new substance formed when two or more ingredients combine.

electron: An atomic particle with a negative charge.

element: A substance made of atoms that all have the same number of protons.

fluid: A type of matter that can flow.

ion: An atom that has a positive or a negative charge.

matter: The basic substance that makes up the universe.

mixture: A combination of two or more ingredients that do not form a new and different substance.

molecule: A tiny particle of matter, too small for the human eye to see. A molecule is the smallest amount of a substance it is possible to have in one place.

neutron: An atomic particle with no charge, which can be found in the nucleus of an atom.

nucleus: The center of an atom, including neutrons and protons.

plasma: A gas consisting of flowing ions and electrons, which conduct electricity.

proton: An atomic particle with a positive charge.

Books

Nick Arnold, *Chemical Chaos*. New York: Scholastic, 1998. Part of Scholastic's Horrible Science series, this book uses cartoons and humor to explain the main concepts used in chemistry.

Christopher Cooper, *Eyewitness: Matter*. New York: Dorling Kindersley, 1999. Three-dimensional illustrations are used to demonstrate basic concepts in chemistry. Molecules, atoms, changes in the state of matter, and the differences between a mixture and a compound are among the topics explained.

Robert Mebane and Thomas Rybolt, *Adventures with Atoms and Molecules: Chemistry Experiments for Young People*. Berkeley Heights, NJ: Enslow, 1998. Chemistry experiments that can be done with household materials.

Robert Snedden, *States of Matter*. Chicago: Heinemann Library, 2001. Includes information about four of the states of matter, as well as the basics of how a molecule is held together.

Web Sites

Chem4Kids (www.chem4kids.com). This site is produced and maintained free by Andrew Rader, a scientist and screenwriter who also produces Star Trek.com. It provides a good basic overview of molecules, atoms, and states of matter, but leaves out Bose-Einstein condensate (BEC).

ScienCentral News: Making Sense of Science (www.sciencentral.com). This Web site includes the latest news about science and technology, including nanotechnology. Features from ScienCentral sometimes appear on ABC and NBC newscasts.

Index

Picture Credits

Cover: © Will and Deni McIntyre/Photo
   Researchers, Inc.
© Art Today, Inc., 12, 19, 24, 31
© COREL Corporation, 31 (inset)
© Brian Doberstein, 12 (inset)
© Macduff Everton/CORBIS, 28–29
© Clive Freeman/Biosym
   Technologies/Photo Researchers, Inc., 8–9
© MARCUS FUEHRER/EPA/Landov, 20
© Roger Harris/Photo Researchers, Inc., 38
© Institute for Experimental Physics,
   University of Innsbruck, 34 (both)
© Laguna Design/Photo Researchers, Inc., 16
© National Institute of Standards and
   Technology (NIST)/Photo Researchers,
   Inc., 33
© Susumu Nishinaga/Photo Researchers,
   Inc., 18
Brandy Noon, 11, 26
© PhotoDisc, 23
© Royalty-Free/CORBIS, 7
© Volker Steger/Sandia National
   Laboratory/Photo Researchers, Inc., 37

About the Author

Bonnie Juettner is a writer and editor of children's reference books and educational videos. Originally from McGrath, Alaska, she currently lives in Kenosha, Wisconsin. This is her sixth book.